Personal Protective Equipment
&
Basic
Fire Extinguisher Usage

(Part of the Security Officers Training Series)

By Timothy Hightshoe

INTRODUCTION

The first part of this booklet is based in part on the Oklahoma State University blood borne pathogen exposure training plan, the blood borne pathogen training plan from the University of Cincinnati and Occupational Safety and Health Administration (OSHA) standards. This program covers the use of personal protective equipment in the security environment. The following pages provide information that can save your life, but should not be considered a comprehensive program.

Not covered in this program is First Aid or Cardiopulmonary Resuscitation (CPR). It is strongly recommended you contact the American Red Cross or the American Heart Association for First Aid and CPR training.

Though every effort has been made to insure accuracy in the information provided, errors may exist and medical technology may discover new information. It is the individual's responsibility to keep current on changes affecting their job. As always, I encourage you to seek continuing education during your career in the security field.

The second part of this booklet is based on the fire prevention program offered by Freetraining.com. It covers the basics of fire safety and the use of fire extinguishers. It is recommended you learn about specific hazards in the location where you are working as well as familiarizing yourself with the specific equipment that may be available to you.

Many local fire departments offer fire safety checks of residences and business as well as training in basic fire prevention and fire fighting techniques.

As always, I encourage you to seek additional training and to continue your training to remain proficient during your career.

Tim Hightshoe

Personal Protective Equipment

BLOOD BORNE PATHOGENS

This booklet is designed to provide a basic understanding of blood borne pathogens, their common modes of transmission, methods of prevention, and other pertinent information.

Since you can reasonably anticipate coming into contact with blood and/or other potentially infectious materials as part of your job duties, it is also recommended that you read OSHA's summary of blood borne pathogens.

Blood borne pathogens are microorganisms such as viruses or bacteria, which are carried in the blood and can cause disease in people. There are many different blood borne pathogens including malaria, syphilis, and brucellosis, but *Hepatitis B (HBV)* and the *Human Immunodeficiency Virus (HIV)* are the two diseases specifically addressed by the OSHA Blood Borne Pathogen Standard.

While this booklet will focus primarily on HBV and HIV, it is important to know which blood borne pathogens (from humans or animals) you may be exposed to through your environment and those you come into contact with.

Hepatitis B (HBV)

In the United States, approximately 300,000 people are infected with HBV annually. Of these cases only a small percentage prove to be fatal. Personnel who are at risk for exposure to Hepatitis B are strongly advised to consult with their physician regarding the HBV vaccination series. More information on the vaccination series will be presented later in the booklet.

Hepatitis means *inflammation of the liver,* and, as its name implies, Hepatitis B is a virus that infects the liver. While there are several different types of Hepatitis, Hepatitis B is transmitted primarily through "blood to blood" contact. Hepatitis B initially causes inflammation of the liver, but it can lead to more serious conditions such as cirrhosis and liver cancer.

There is no "cure" or specific treatment for HBV, but many people who contract the disease will develop antibodies, which can help them get over the infection and protect them from getting it again. It is important to note however, that there are different kinds of hepatitis, so antibodies from HBV will not prevent someone from getting one of the other varieties.

The Hepatitis B virus is very durable, and can survive in dried blood for up to seven days. For this reason, this virus is a serious concern for security officers, custodians, laundry personnel and others who may come in contact with blood or potentially infectious materials in a non First Aid or medical care situation.

Symptoms:

The symptoms of HBV are very much like a mild "flu". Initially, there is a feeling of fatigue, possible stomach pain, loss of appetite, and even nausea. As the disease continues to develop, jaundice (a distinct yellowing of the skin and eyes), and darkened urine will often occur. However, people who are infected with HBV will often show no symptoms for quite some time. After exposure it can take **1-9 months** before symptoms become noticeable. Loss of appetite and stomach pain, for example, commonly appear within 1-3 months, but can occur as soon as 2 weeks or as long as 6-9 months after infection.

Hepatitis C (HCV)

There is no vaccine available for HCV. The risk of acquiring an infection following exposure is approximately 2-3 %. In 1996 there were approximately 36,000 new HCV infections in the U.S. In more than 85% of infected persons, chronic infection will occur. 8,000 – 10,000 deaths occur annually.

Human Immunodeficiency Virus (HIV)

AIDS, or Acquired Immune Deficiency Syndrome, is caused by a virus called the Human Immunodeficiency Virus, or HIV. Once a person has been infected with HIV, it may be many years before AIDS actually develops. HIV attacks the body's immune system, weakening it so it cannot fight other deadly diseases. AIDS is a fatal disease, and, while treatment for it is improving, there is no known cure.

Estimates on the number of people infected with HIV vary, but some estimates suggest an average of 35,000 people are infected every year in the US (in 2000, 45,000 new infections were reported). It is believed that as of 2000, 920,000 persons were living with HIV / AIDS in the United States. These numbers could be higher, as many people who are infected with HIV may be completely unaware of it.

While the HIV virus is very fragile and will not survive for long outside of the human body, it is still of concern to employees providing First Aid or medical care in situations involving fresh blood or other potentially infectious materials. It is estimated the chances of contracting HIV in a workplace environment are only 0.4%. However, because it is such a devastating disease, all precautions must be taken to avoid exposure.

AIDS infection essentially occurs in three broad stages. The first stage happens when a person is actually infected with HIV. After the initial infection, a person may show few or no signs of illness for many years. Eventually, in the second stage, an individual may begin to suffer swollen lymph glands or other lesser diseases, which begin to take advantage of the body's weakened immune system. The second stage is believed to eventually lead to AIDS, the third and final stage. In this stage, the body becomes completely unable to fight off life-threatening diseases and infections.

Symptoms:

Symptoms of HIV infection can vary, but often include weakness, fever, sore throat, nausea, headaches, diarrhea, a white coating on the tongue, weight loss, and swollen lymph glands.

If you believe you have been exposed to HBV or HIV, especially if you have experienced any of the signs or symptoms of these diseases, you should consult your physician or doctor as soon as possible.

MODES OF TRANSMISSION

Blood borne pathogens such as HBV and HIV can be transmitted through contact with infected human blood and other potentially infectious body fluids such as:

- Semen
- Vaginal secretions
- Cerebrospinal fluid
- Synovial fluid
- Pleural fluid
- Peritoneal fluid
- Amniotic fluid
- Saliva
- Any body fluid that is visibly contaminated with blood

It is important to know the ways exposure and transmission are most likely to occur in your particular situation, be it from providing First Aid, cleaning up blood after an incident, or contact with potentially infectious materials during a physical altercation.

HBV and HIV are most commonly transmitted through:

- Sexual Contact.
- Sharing of hypodermic needles
- From mother to baby at/before birth
- Accidental puncture from contaminated needles, broken glass, or other sharps.
- Contact between broken or damaged skin and infected body fluids
- Contact between mucous membranes and infected body fluids

Accidental punctures from contaminated needles and other sharps can result in transmission of blood borne pathogens.

In most security work, transmission is most likely to occur because of an accidental puncture from contaminated needles, broken glass, or other sharps; contact between broken or damaged skin and infected body fluids or contact between mucous membranes and infected body fluids. For example: if someone infected with HBV cut his or her finger on a piece of glass then you cut yourself on the now infected piece of glass, it is possible you could contract the disease. Anytime there is blood-to-blood contact with infected blood or body fluids, there is a potential for transmission.

Unbroken skin forms an impervious barrier against blood borne pathogens. However, infected blood can enter your system through:

- Open sores
- Cuts (small cuts or breaks in the skin are very dangerous as you may or may not even know you have one)
- Abrasions
- Acne
- Any sort of damaged or broken skin, such as sunburn or blisters

Blood borne pathogens may also be transmitted through the mucous membranes of the:

- Eyes
- Nose
- Mouth

For example, a splash of contaminated blood to your eyes, nose, or mouth could result in transmission.

PERSONAL PROTECTIVE EQUIPMENT & WORK PRACTICES

It is extremely important to use personal protective equipment and work practice controls to protect yourself from blood borne pathogens.

Universal Precautions is the name used to describe a prevention strategy in which all blood and potentially infectious materials are treated as if they are, in fact, infectious, regardless of the perceived status of the source individual. In other words, whether or not you think the blood/body fluid is infected with blood borne pathogens, *you treat it as if it is*. This approach is used in all situations where exposure to blood or potentially infectious materials is possible. This also means that certain work practice controls should *always* be utilized in situations where exposure may occur.

Personal Protective Equipment

Probably the first thing to do in any situation where you may be exposed to blood borne pathogens is to ensure you are wearing the appropriate personal protective equipment (PPE). For example, you may have noticed that emergency medical personnel, doctors, nurses, dentists, dental assistants, and other health care professionals always wear latex or protective gloves. This is a simple precaution they take in order to prevent blood or potentially infectious body fluids from coming in contact with their skin.

To protect yourself, it is essential to have a barrier between you and the potentially infectious material.

Rules to follow:

- Always wear PPE in potential exposure situations.
- Remove PPE that is torn or punctured, or has lost its ability to function as a barrier to blood borne pathogens
- Replace PPE that is torn or punctured

Since we do not know when an exposure to blood or potentially infectious materials may occur, the necessary PPE should be readily accessible. Contaminated gloves, clothing, PPE, or other materials should be placed in appropriately labeled bags or containers until they can be disposed of, decontaminated or laundered. It is important to find out where these bags or containers are located in your area before beginning your work.

Gloves should be made of latex, nitrile, rubber, or other water impervious materials. If glove material is thin or flimsy, double gloving can provide an additional layer of protection. Also, if you know you have cuts or sores on your hands, you should cover these with a bandage or similar protection as an additional precaution before donning your gloves.

You should always inspect your gloves for tears or punctures before putting them on and at least weekly if carried on your duty belt or other areas where damage can occur.
If a glove is damaged, don't use it!

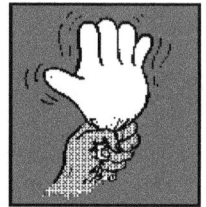

When taking contaminated gloves off, do so carefully. Make sure you don't touch the outside of the gloves with any bare skin, and be sure to dispose of them in a proper container so that no one else will come in contact with them, either. It is also recommended that gloves be removed in a manner that turns them inside out before disposal.

Face shields, glasses or goggles may be worn to provide eye and face protection. A face shield will protect against splashes to the nose and mouth, which glasses or goggles will not.

Aprons may be worn to protect your clothing and to keep blood or other contaminated fluids from soaking through to your skin.

8

Normal clothing that becomes contaminated with blood should be removed as soon as possible as fluids can seep through the cloth and come into contact with skin. Contaminated laundry should be handled as little as possible and should be placed in an appropriately labeled bag or container until it can be decontaminated, disposed of, or laundered.

Remember to use universal precautions and treat all blood or potentially infectious body fluids as if they are contaminated. Avoid contact whenever possible, and always wear personal protective equipment.

If you find yourself in a situation where you have to come in contact with blood or other body fluids and you don't have any standard PPE equipment handy, you can improvise. Use a towel, plastic bag, or some other barrier to help avoid direct contact.

HYGIENE PRACTICES

Hand washing is one of the most important (and easiest) practices used to prevent transmission of blood borne pathogens. Hands or other exposed skin should be thoroughly washed as soon as possible following an exposure incident. Use soft, antibacterial soap, if possible. Avoid harsh, abrasive soaps, as these may open fragile scabs or other sores.

Hands should also be washed immediately (or as soon as feasible) after removal of gloves or other personal protective equipment.

Because hand washing is so important, you should familiarize yourself with the location of the hand washing facilities nearest to you. Public restrooms, janitor closets, and so forth may be used for hand washing if they are normally supplied with soap. If you are working in an area without access to such facilities, you may use an antiseptic cleanser such as Purell® Hand Sanitizer in conjunction with clean cloth/paper towels or antiseptic towelettes. If these alternative methods are used, hands should be washed with soap and running water as soon as possible.

If you are working in an area where there is reasonable likelihood of exposure, you should never:

- Eat
- Drink
- Smoke
- Apply cosmetics or lip balm
- Handle contact lenses

DECONTAMINATION AND STERILIZATION

All surfaces, tools, equipment and other objects that come in contact with blood or potentially infectious materials must be decontaminated and sterilized as soon as possible. Equipment and tools must be cleaned and decontaminated before servicing or being put back to use.

Decontamination should be accomplished by using:

- A solution of 5.25% sodium hypochlorite (household bleach / Clorox®) diluted between 1:10 and 1:100 with water. The standard recommendation is to use at least a quarter cup of bleach per one gallon of water.
- Lysol or some other EPA-registered tuberculocidal disinfectant.

Check the label of all disinfectants to make sure they meet this requirement.

If you are cleaning up blood, you should carefully cover the blood with paper towels or rags (if available), then gently pour the diluted solution of bleach over the towels or rags, and leave it for *at least 10 minutes*. This will help ensure that any blood borne pathogens are killed before you actually begin cleaning or wiping the material up. By covering the spill with paper towels or rags, you decrease the chances of causing a splash when you pour the bleach on it.

If you are decontaminating equipment or other objects (be it handcuffs, batons, vehicles, First Aid boxes, etc.) you should leave the disinfectant in place for *at least 10 minutes* before continuing the cleaning process.

Of course, any materials you use to clean up a spill of blood or potentially infectious materials must be decontaminated immediately, as well. This includes mops, sponges, re-usable gloves, buckets, pails, etc.

Sharps

Far too frequently, security officers and others are punctured or cut by improperly disposed needles and broken glass. This, of course, exposes them to whatever infectious material may have been on the glass or needle. For this reason, it is especially important to handle and dispose of all sharps carefully in order to protect yourself as well as others.

Needles

- Needles should never be recapped.
- Needles should be moved only by using a mechanical device or tool such as forceps, pliers or broom and dustpan.
- Never break or shear needles.

Broken Glassware

- Broken glassware that has been visibly contaminated with blood must be sterilized with an approved disinfectant solution before it is disturbed or cleaned up.
- Glassware that has been decontaminated may be disposed of in an appropriate sharps container: closable, puncture resistance, leak-proof on sides and bottom and labeled appropriately.
- Uncontaminated broken glassware may be disposed of in a closable, puncture resistant container such as a cardboard box or coffee can.

By using Universal Precautions and following these simple work practices, you can protect yourself and prevent transmission of blood borne pathogens.

SIGNS, LABELS & COLOR CODING

Warning labels need to be affixed to containers of regulated waste, refrigerators and freezers containing blood or other potentially infectious material; and other containers used to store, transport, or ship blood or other potentially infectious materials. These labels should be fluorescent orange, red, or orange-red. Bags used to dispose of regulated waste must be red or orange-red and must have the biohazard symbol readily visible upon them. Regulated waste should be double-bagged to guard against the possibility of leakage if the first bag is punctured.

Labels should display this universal biohazard symbol.

Regulated waste refers to:

- Any liquid or semi-liquid blood or other potentially infectious materials.
- Contaminated items that would release blood or other potentially infectious materials in a liquid or semi-liquid state if compressed.
- Items that are caked with dried blood or other potentially infectious materials and are capable of releasing these materials during handling.
- Contaminated sharps.
- Pathological and microbiological wastes containing blood or other potentially infectious materials.

All regulated waste must be disposed of in properly labeled containers or red biohazard bags, and must be disposed at an approved facility. Most ambulances or police departments will have some sort of contract with an outside disposal company that will pick up their waste and take it to an approved incineration/disposal facility. Security officers should not handle regulated waste if at all possible.

Non-regulated waste (i.e., does not fit the definition of regulated waste provided above) may be disposed in regular plastic trash bags *if it has been decontaminated prior to disposal.*

Emergency Procedures

In an emergency situation involving blood or potentially infectious materials, you should always use Universal Precautions and try to minimize your exposure by wearing gloves, splash goggles, pocket mouth-to-mouth resuscitation masks, and other barrier devices.

If you are exposed, however, you should:

1. Wash the exposed area thoroughly with soap and running water. Use non-abrasive, antibacterial soap if possible. If blood is splashed in the eyes or mucous membranes, flush the affected area with running water for at least 15 minutes.

2. Report the exposure to your supervisor as soon as possible.

3. Fill out an exposure report, so that you can document workplace exposure to hazardous substances. Your report should included the following:

    *   The route(s) of exposure and the circumstances under which the exposure incident occurred.
    *   Identify and document the source individual unless such documentation is impossible or prohibited by law.

4. After exposure, you should request the following from your company:

- Have the source individual's blood tested for HBV and HIV as soon as possible after consent is obtained. If the source individual is known to be seropositive for HBV or HIV, testing for that virus need not be done.
- Have your blood collected as soon feasible, and tested after your consent is obtained.
- When medically indicated, administer post exposure prophylaxes, as recommended by the US Public Health Service.
- Get counseling.
- Have all illnesses evaluated.
- Apart from the circumstances surrounding the exposure itself, all other findings or diagnosis should remain entirely confidential.

HEPATITIS B VACCINATIONS

Employees who have routine exposure to blood borne pathogens (security officers, first responders, etc) shall be offered the Hepatitis B vaccine series at no cost to themselves (OSHA requirement) unless:

- They have previously received the vaccine series.
- Antibody testing has revealed they are immune.
- The vaccine is contraindicated for medical reasons.

Although your employer must offer the vaccine to you, you do not have to accept that offer. You may opt to decline the vaccination series, in which case you should be asked to sign a declination form. **Even if you decline the initial offer, you may choose to receive the series at anytime during your employment thereafter**. For example, if you are exposed on the job at a later date. Even if the vaccine is administered immediately after exposure it has proven very effective at preventing the disease.

The Hepatitis B vaccination is given in a series of three shots. The second shot is given one month after the first, and the third shot follows five months after the second. This series gradually builds up the body's immunity to the Hepatitis B virus.

The vaccine itself is made from yeast cultures; there is no risk of contracting the disease from getting the shots and once vaccinated, a person does not need to receive the series again. There are booster shots available however, and in some instances these may be recommended (for example: if there is an outbreak of Hepatitis B at a particular location).

FINAL THOUGHTS

PPE equipment will not prevent the transmission of pathogens if left in the trunk of your patrol car. Likewise, gloves left in a pouch on your duty belt will not work either.

BLOOD BORNE PATHOGENS SELF TEST

1. If you are exposed to potentially infectious materials on the job, you may request a vaccine for which blood borne disease?

    A. HIV
    B. Syphilis
    C. Hepatitis B
    D. Brucellosis

2. Which of the following materials could contain blood borne pathogens?

    A. Bloody saliva
    B. Semen
    C. Vaginal secretions
    D. All of the above

3. If you wear gloves when cleaning up an accident site, it is not necessary to wash your hands afterwards.

    A. True
    B. False

4. Blood borne pathogens may enter your system through:

    A. Open cuts
    B. Skin abrasions
    C. Dermatitis
    D. Mucous membranes
    E. All of the Above

5. You should always treat all body fluids as if they are infectious and avoid direct contact with them.

    A. True
    B. False

6. You should never eat, drink or smoke in any area where there may be potential exposure to blood borne pathogens.

    A. True
    B. False

7. If you have blood or potentially infectious materials splashed into your eye, you should flush your eyes with clean, running water for...

    A. 2 minutes
    B. 5 minutes
    C. 10 minutes
    D. 15 minutes

8. Uncontaminated sharps may be disposed of in regular trash bags

    A. True
    B. False

9. A quarter cup of household bleach to one gallon of water provides a strong enough solution to effectively decontaminate most surfaces, tools and equipment if left for ten minutes.

    A. True
    B. False

10. Needles should never by recapped.

    A. True
    B. False

FIRE BASICS

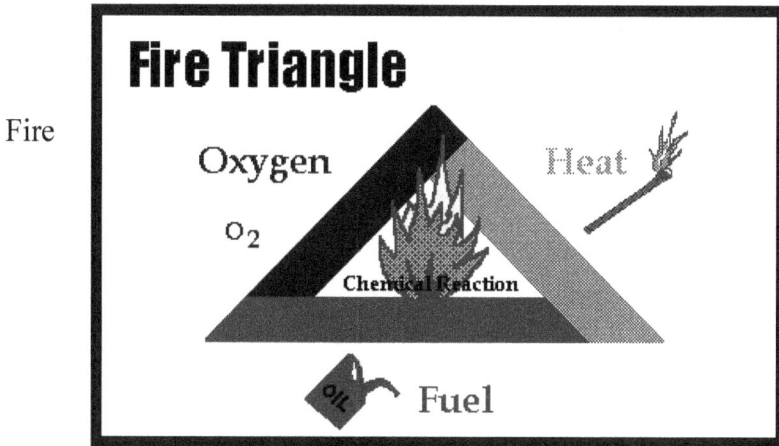

Fire safety, at its most basic, is based upon the principle of keeping fuel sources and ignition sources separate.

Three things must be present at the same time to produce fire:

1.   Enough Oxygen to sustain combustion

2.   Enough Heat to reach ignition temperature

3.   Some Fuel or combustible material

Together, they produce the chemical reaction that is fire. Take away any of these things and the fire will be extinguished.

FUEL CLASSIFICATIONS

Fires are classified according to the type of fuel that is burning. If you use the wrong type of extinguisher on the wrong class of fire, you can make matters worse. It is very important to understand the four different fire (fuel) classifications:

 Class A: Wood, paper, cloth, trash, plastics—solids that are not metals.

 Class B: Flammable liquids—gasoline, oil, grease, acetone. Includes flammable gases.

 Class C: Electrical—energized electrical equipment. As long as it is "plugged in."

 Class D: Metals—potassium, sodium, aluminum, magnesium. Requires Metal-X, foam, and other special extinguishing agents.

Most fire extinguishers will have a pictograph label telling you which type of fire they are designed to fight.

For example, a simple water extinguisher might have a label like this, which means it should only be used on Class A fires.

TYPES OF FIRE EXTINGUISHERS

Different types of fire extinguishers are designed to fight different classes of fire. The most common types of fire extinguishers are:

1. Water (Air Pressurized Water)

Large, silver fire extinguishers that stand about 2 feet tall and weigh about 25 pounds when full.

APW stands for "Air-Pressurized Water." Filled with ordinary tap water and pressurized air, they are essentially large squirt guns.

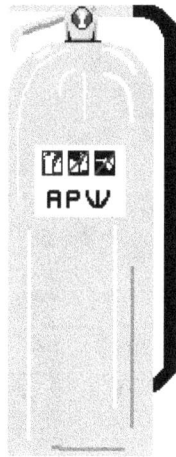

Will have gauge

↓ Air ↓

Water

APW APW

APW's extinguish fire by taking away the "Heat" element of the Fire Triangle. They are designed for Class A fires **only**: Wood, paper, cloth. Here are a few of the reasons you need to be careful about which extinguisher you use:

- Using water on a flammable liquid fire can cause the fire to spread.
- Using water on an electrical fire increases the risk of

electrocution. If you have no choice but to use an APW on an electrical fire, make sure the electrical equipment is unplugged or de-energized.

APW's can usually be found in older buildings, particularly in public hallways.

2.   Carbon Dioxide (CO2)

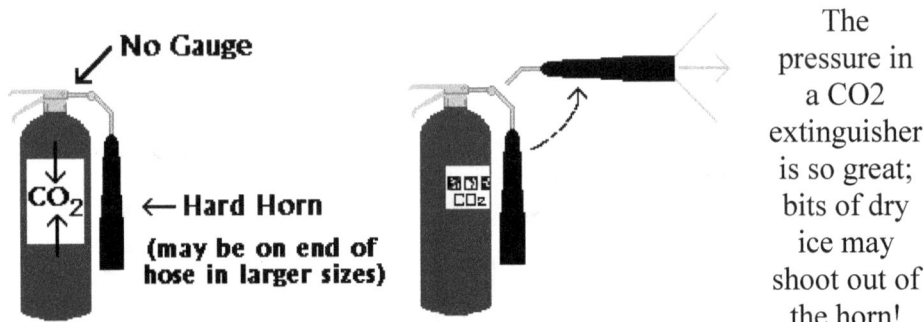

The pressure in a CO2 extinguisher is so great; bits of dry ice may shoot out of the horn!

No Gauge

← **Hard Horn**
(may be on end of hose in larger sizes)

CO2 cylinders are red. They range in size from 5 pounds to 100 pounds or larger. On larger sizes, the horn will be at the end of a long, flexible hose.

CO2's are designed for Class B and C (flammable liquids and electrical sources) fires only!

CO2's will frequently be found in laboratories, mechanical rooms, kitchens, and flammable liquid storage areas.

In accordance with National Fire Protection Association (NFPA) regulations (and manufacturers' recommendations) all CO2 extinguishers must undergo hydrostatic testing and recharge every five years.

Carbon dioxide is a non-flammable gas that takes away the oxygen element of the fire triangle. CO2 is very cold as it comes out of the extinguisher, so it cools the fuel as well.

A CO2 extinguisher may *not* be very effective in extinguishing a Class

A fire because it may not be able to displace enough oxygen to successfully put the fire out. Class A materials can also smolder and re-ignite.

3.   Dry Chemical (ABC, BC, DC)

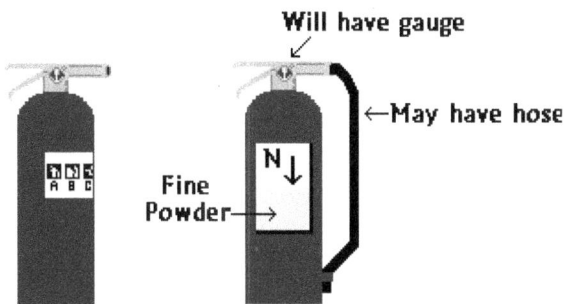

ABC extinguishers are red. They can range in size from five pounds to 20 pounds.

Most ABC extinguishers are filled with a fine, yellow powder. This powder is primarily composed of monoammonium phosphate. The extinguishers are pressurized with nitrogen. Dry chemical extinguishers put out fire by coating the fuel with a thin layer of dust. This separates the fuel from the oxygen in the air. The powder also works to interrupt the chemical reaction of fire. These extinguishers are very effective at putting out fire. Dry chemical extinguishers come in a variety of types. You may see them labeled:

- DC (for dry chemical)
- ABC (can be used on Class A, B or C fires)
- BC (designed for use on Class B and C fires)

It is extremely important to identify which types of dry chemical fire extinguishers are located in your area! You don't want to mistakenly use a "BC" extinguisher on a Class A fire thinking it was an "ABC" extinguisher.

An "ABC" extinguisher will have a label like this, indicating it may be used on Class A, B, and C fires.

Dry chemical extinguishers with powder designed for Class B and C fires ("BC" extinguishers) may be located in places such as commercial kitchens and areas with flammable liquids.

You will usually find ABC's in public hallways of new buildings, in laboratories, break rooms, offices, chemical storage areas, mechanical rooms, vehicles, etc.

HOW TO USE A FIRE EXTINGUISHER

It is easy to remember how to use a fire extinguisher if you remember the acronym, "PASS."

Pull
Aim
Squeeze
Sweep

Pull the pin. This will allow you to discharge the extinguisher.	**Pull** the pin
Aim at the base of the fire. Hit the fuel…if you aim at the flames, the extinguishing agent will pass right through and do no good.	
Squeeze the top handle. This depresses a button that releases the pressurized extinguishing agent.	**Squeeze ↓** the handle
Sweep from side-to-side until the fire is completely out. Start using the extinguisher from a safe distance away and then slowly move forward. Once the fire is out, keep an eye on the area in case it re-ignites.	**Sweep** side to side

IMPORTANT RULES TO REMEMBER

Fires can be very dangerous and you should always be certain you will not endanger yourself or others when attempting to put out a fire. For this reason, when a fire is discovered:

1. Most fires start small. Except for explosions, fires can usually by brought under control if they are attacked correctly with the right type and size of extinguisher within the first two minutes!

2. A fire extinguisher should be "listed and labeled" by an independent testing laboratory. The higher the rating number on an A or B or C extinguisher, the more fire it can put out. Be careful, high-rated units are often heavier models. Make sure you can hold and operate the model you are buying.

3. A portable fire extinguisher can save lives and property by putting out a small fire or containing it until the fire department arrives. Before attempting to fight a *small* fire be sure everyone is out of the building. It is important to have someone call the fire department. If the fire starts to spread or threatens your escape path, *get out immediately!*

4. The operator must know how to use the extinguisher, quickly without taking time to read directions during an emergency. Remember that the extinguishers need care and must be recharged after every use.

WHEN NOT TO FIGHT A FIRE...

- If the fire could block your only exit!

- If the fire is spreading too quickly!

- If the type or size of the extinguisher is wrong!

- If the fire is too large!

- If you don't know how to use your fire extinguisher!

If any of the above conditions exist, leave immediately!!!

As you evacuate a building, close doors and windows behind you as you leave.

This will help to slow the spread of smoke and fire.

The final rule to remember is: always position yourself with an exit or means of escape at your back before you attempt to use an extinguisher to put out a fire.

In case the extinguisher malfunctions, or something unexpected happens, you need to be able to get out quickly. You don't want to become trapped.

FIRE EXTINGUISHER SELF TEST

1. Examples of two "Class B' fuels would be plastic and grease.

    A. True
    B. False

2. An APW (water extinguisher) is safe to use on an electrical fire.

    A. True
    B. False

3. Carbon Dioxide extinguishers are designed for which types of fuels?

    A. Class B and C
    B. Class A, B and C
    C. Class A and C
    D. Class A and B

4. Which type of extinguisher has a hard horn on the end of a flexible hose or metal arm?

    A. APW (air-pressurized water)
    B. CO2 (carbon dioxide)
    C. ABC (dry chemical)

5. As a general rule, you should not attempt to fight a fire if it is spreading rapidly.

    A. True
    B. False

6. ABC fire extinguishers extinguish fire by cooling it down.

    A. True
    B. False

7. Water will not extinguish most flammable liquid fires.

   A. True
   B. False

8. You should always keep an exit or means of escape at your back when trying to fight a fire.

   A. True
   B. False

9. The three elements of the fire triangle are:

   A. Water, a heat source, and fuel
   B. Oxygen, water, and fuel
   C. Oxygen, fuel, and a heat source
   D. Fuel, oxygen, and earth

10. Do you know where the nearest fire extinguisher is in your work area?

   A. Yes
   B. No

Answer key for Self Test - Personal Protection Equipment

1. C
2. D
3. B
4. E
5. A
6. A
7. D
8. B
9. A
10. A

Answer key to Self Test - Basic Fire Extinguisher

1. B
2. B
3. A
4. B
5. A
6. A
7. A
8. A
9. C
10. The correct answer should be A. however, if you answered B, then you should take the time to locate the nearest fire extinguisher and familiarize yourself with its use.

Timothy Hightshoe:

Front Range International Defensive Pistol Association (IDPA) President // Safety Officer and Match Conduct Instructor // Peace Officer Standards and Training Board (P.O.S.T.) Certified Handgun Instructor // USAF (Colorado Air National Guard) Combat Arms Instructor // Defensive Handgun, Long gun Training Association (DeHLTA) Co-founder and Rifle/Pistol/Shotgun Instructor // Aurora Community College P.O.S.T. Handgun At-Will Instructor // Graduated from Denny Chalker's (Command Master Chief, Ret., SEAL Team 6) Executive Protection (knife/hand/gun) Training // Graduated Gun Sight Pistol/Carbine/Shotgun training // Completed Matt Burkett's Practical Hand Gunning course. // Veteran of Desert Storm / Desert Shield / Noble Eagle // Trained troops for Operations Just Cause / Enduring Freedom / Iraqi Freedom.

www.ingramcontent.com/pod-product-compliance
Lightning Source LLC
Chambersburg PA
CBHW060705280326
41933CB00012B/2313